New Moms
Need New Swear Words!

A FUN NEW COLORING BOOK!

by
JD Clean Swears Coloring

New Moms Need New Swear Words!: A Fun New Coloring Book!
by JD Clean Swears Coloring

Cover and interior images copyright: olich15 and hurca.com. Used under License from Adobe Stock (stock.adobe.com) – Extended Licenses purchased where necessary. Merienda One font: Copyright (c) 2011, Eduardo Tunni (http://www.tipo.net.ar), used under the SIL Open Font License, Version 1.1. Pacifico font: Copyright (c) 2011, Vernon Adams (vern@newtypography.co.uk), used under the SIL Open Font License, Version 1.1.

Copyright © 2016 Dr Jason Davies
All rights reserved. No part of this publication may be reproduced, stored in a retrieval system, or transmitted in any form or by any means, electronic, mechanical, photocopying, recording or otherwise, without the prior written permission of the publisher.

ISBN-13: 978-1534871915
ISBN-10: 1534871918

Made in the USA
Monee, IL
17 March 2021